Speaking Frames

Year 5

Sue Palmer

shers

David Fulton Publishers Ltd
The Chiswick Centre, 414 Chiswick High Road, London W4 5TF

www.fultonpublishers.co.uk

First published in 2004 in Great Britain by David Fulton Publishers

10 9 8 7 6 5 4 3 2

David Fulton Publishers is a division of Granada Learning, part of Granada plc.

Note: The right of Sue Palmer to be identified as the author of this work has been asserted by her in accordance with the Copyright, Designs and Patents Act 1988.

Copyright © Sue Palmer 2004

British Library Cataloguing in Publication Data
A catalogue record for this book is available from the British Library.

ISBN 1-8431-2-111-5

Designed and typeset by Kenneth Burnle
Printed and bound in Great Britain

CONTENTS

Related titles of interest

Word Power: Activities for Years 3 and 4
Terry Saunders
1-8431-2141-7
c. £12.00
Publication February 2004

Word Power: Activities for Years 5 and 6
Terry Saunders
1-8431-2142-5
c. £12.00
Publication February 2004

Writing Models – Year 3
Pie Corbett
1-8431-2094-1
Publication 2004

Writing Models – Year 4
Pie Corbett
1-8431-2095-X
Publication 2004

Writing Models – Year 5
Pie Corbett
1-8431-2096-8
Publication 2004

Writing Models – Year 6
Pie Corbett
1-8431-2097-6
Publication 2004

INTRODUCING SPEAKING FRAMES

Speaking frames are frameworks for directed speaking and listening activities in the primary classroom. They are specifically designed to help pupils move on from the restricted patterns of spoken language to the more complex patterns of written language and 'literate talk'. In this way, it is hoped they will help develop children's control over language in both speaking and writing.

Spoken and written language patterns

It is now well established that written language is very different from the spoken variety. Speech is generally interactive – we bat words and phrases back and forth – and produced within a shared context, so it's fragmented and disorganised, and a great deal of meaning goes by 'on the nod'. In fact, you can get by in speech without ever forming a sentence, or at least only very simple ones. To make links between ideas, speakers tend to use very simple connectives, such as the ubiquitous *and* or, to denote sequence, *and then*. This kind of language is described by linguists as 'spontaneous speech'.

On the other hand, written language is produced for an unknown, unseen audience, who may have no background knowledge at all about the subject. It must therefore be explicit and carefully crafted. It requires more extensive vocabulary than speech and organisation into sentences for clarity. The sentences become increasingly complex as the writer expresses increasingly complex ideas, using a widening range of connectives to show how these ideas relate to each other.

The interface between speech and writing

The more 'literate' someone is, the more written language patterns begin to inform their speech. Exposure to literate language through reading, and the opportunity to develop control of it oneself through writing, leads to increasingly literate spoken language. It seems to be a cyclical process: speech informs writing, which then informs speech, which informs writing, and so on. In general, the more accomplished the writer, the better equipped he or she is to 'talk like a book'.

Until the late nineteenth century, this interface between speech and writing was universally acknowledged. From the time of the Ancient Greeks, **rhetoric** (reading aloud, speaking persuasively) was considered as essential a part of education as reading and writing – perhaps even more so. Exercises in rhetoric were intended to develop not only pupils' powers of oratory, but also their ear for language – the explicit, complex patterns of language in which educated people converse and write. As Ben Jonson put it in 1640: 'For a man to write well, there are required three necessaries: to read the best authors, to hear the best speakers, and much exercise of his own style.'

However, the introduction of universal state education meant large classes in which speech for the many was not deemed possible (or desirable), and the literacy curriculum was restricted to reading and writing. Throughout the twentieth century, educators concentrated their attention on literacy, at the expense of oracy. Speaking frames provide a twenty-first-century approach to the forgotten 'fourth R'.

The 'two horses' model

Speaking frames were initially developed as an aid to writing. Teaching children to write without first giving opportunities to speak is, fairly obviously, 'putting the cart before the horse.' However, opportunities for talk before writing do not necessarily develop literate language patterns. Ideally, there should be two 'oracy horses' drawing the 'writing cart'.

The first is a text-level horse – dealing with 'talk for learning'. These spoken language activities are vital for helping children to:

- engage with the subject under discussion
- familiarise themselves with key vocabulary
- get to grips with underlying concepts
- organise their ideas appropriately before they write.

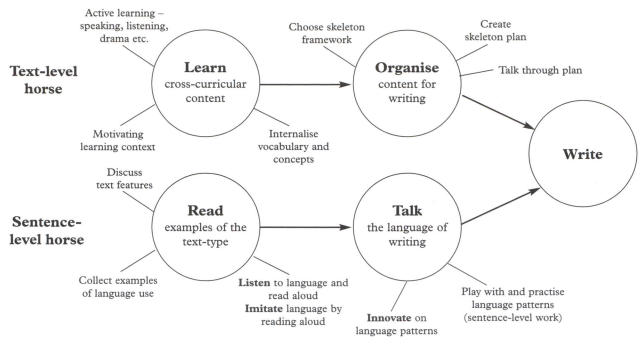

Figure 1: Two horses before the cart

The talk will generally be interactive, context-dependent and conducted in the language of spontaneous speech. There are many suggestions for providing 'talk for learning' in *How to Teach Writing Across the Curriculum at Key Stage 2* (Palmer 2001) and *How to Teach Writing Across the Curriculum at Key Stage 1* (Palmer 2002).

The second is a sentence-level horse – developing 'talk for writing'. This gives the opportunity for children to develop knowledge about and familiarity with the sorts of language appropriate to the writing task. Speaking frames were developed as a means of focusing on elements of literate language by which ideas can be expressed clearly and coherently for an unknown audience.

Listen – Imitate – Innovate – Invent

There is a well-established developmental model for the way children acquire speech: first they **listen** to adult speakers and **imitate** elements of their speech; then they begin to **innovate** on these language patterns; finally they use all this language data to **invent** their own expressions. However, in terms of acquiring written language patterns – which are, indeed, much more demanding in terms of form and complexity – we make little provision for the first three stages. All too often, we ask children to go straight to invention.

For children with a strong background of literacy this may not be a problem. If they come from families where 'literate talk' is the norm, they may well absorb and reproduce many of its features as naturally as we all acquire spontaneous speech patterns. It therefore pays to be born into a language-rich home! There is another group of children who are likely to absorb written language patterns without effort, whatever their social background. These are the ones who learn to read easily, and who then become committed readers, tackling a wide range of reading matter. They'll pick up written language patterns through frequent exposure to the printed page. However, in a multimedia world, where children can access all the entertainment and information they want via visual displays on a screen, fewer and fewer of them are reading widely in their leisure time. For the majority of children, unless we provide structured help, learning to write will be inhibited by a lack of appropriate vocabulary, language constructions and cohesive devices.

Integrating 'Listen – Imitate – Innovate – Invent' into teaching

Most teachers now spend time before children write in familiarising them with key aspects of the particular text-type – building up a 'writer's toolkit' of organisational and linguistic features. Many of these language patterns are unfamiliar to children and opportunities to listen, imitate and innovate can develop familiarity and help children internalise the linguistic features so that they are available both for writing and for literate talk.

- **Listen** Children need opportunities to *hear* literate language as often as possible, to become familiar with the rhythms and patterns of sentences, and of specific phrases and constructions that are particularly useful for a text-type.
- **Imitate** They also need the chance to produce literate language patterns from their own mouths – to know how more sophisticated vocabulary and phraseology *feel*, and to respond physically to the ebb and flow of well-constructed sentences.
- **Innovate** Then they need opportunities to innovate on those patterns, expressing their own ideas and understanding through the medium of literate talk.

One way of ensuring children **listen to** and **imitate** written language patterns is through reading aloud to them and ensuring that they have plenty of opportunities to read aloud themselves (paired reading with a partner – one paragraph each – is a good way of ensuring the latter). However, it is difficult to target specific language patterns in this way, and reading aloud does not provide an opportunity to **innovate**.

How speaking frames work

Speaking frames replicate the listen–imitate–innovate model for specific types of language as part of children's learning across the curriculum. In pairs, in groups or as individuals, pupils work on specific tasks and fit their answers into a given frame for oral presentation to the class. The class therefore **listens** to a number of presentations based on the frame:

- first by the teacher, as he or she demonstrates the process
- next by more able pupils, selected by the teacher as likely to provide good and fluent models
- then by their remaining peers.

And every child has an opportunity to **imitate** and **innovate** on the same language patterns as they make their own presentation.

Nine specific speaking frames are provided, as a starting point for teachers and pupils. There is also a 'smorgasbord' of useful sentence starts relating to the sorts of talking and writing children need in Year 5. Teachers can use these as they are (according to the notes supplied with each photocopiable page) or take from them to make further speaking frames based on the cross-curricular work or literacy objectives being pursued by the class.

The importance of literate talk

Although speaking frames were originally devised to help children get to grips with written language, their potential use in the development of children's oral language skills is perhaps even more important. The frames facilitate the virtuous circle described above whereby 'speech informs writing . . . informs speech . . . informs writing . . . informs speech . . .', and thus should help develop children's powers of literate speech as much they develop written work. The sooner we can help make children familiar and comfortable with the patterns of literate talk the better. As Thomas Jefferson put it: 'Style, in writing or speaking, is formed very early in life, when the imagination is warm and impressions are permanent.'

Many children find speaking in front of an audience difficult, often because they do not have access to the patterns of literate talk. Trapped in spontaneous spoken language patterns, their vocabulary is limited and speech is fragmented, incoherent and lacking in organisation. Speaking frames provide support in translating their ideas into coherent sentences, and preparing their presentation gives the time to consider vocabulary, develop explicitness and experiment with more formal connectives than they would usually use. Practice makes perfect, and the opportunities provided here to practise presentation skills should also develop children's confidence, social skills and self-esteem.

The speaking frames provided are for three types of presentation: children working in pairs, as individuals and in groups of around six. Each type of presentation requires preliminary teaching, which can be covered using the three sample frames.

A note on assessment

Speaking and listening are notoriously difficult to assess, and this is particularly the case with 'talk for writing', where many social, intellectual and linguistic subskills are brought together in reaching the final presentation. This book breaks the pupil's performance into four elements, covered in two teaching sections.

Section 1: Introducing the activity
  • **preparation** for the presentation
  • the **content** of the presentation.

Section 2: Staging the presentation
  • specific **language** use in the presentation (moving towards literate language)
  • **presentation** skills.

Because so many skills are involved, it is difficult to be precise about teaching objectives. Teachers will obviously concentrate on objectives as appropriate to the ability and experience of pupils. However, too much emphasis on specific objectives here could lead to very reductionist teaching. The activities cover many aspects of the literacy curriculum as well as cross-curricular thinking skills, social skills and the development of self-esteem. The true learning objective is the orchestration of all these skills in pursuit of a clearly defined outcome: the presentation itself. While the teacher may choose to emphasise a particular aspect of any of the four elements listed above, it should always be seen within the context of the whole activity.

Simple assessment sheets are provided for each of the types of presentation, to help teachers focus on the performance of specific children, pairs or groups. Another means of assessment is to video or audio-tape children's presentations and let them assess their own performance, using the *Giving the talk* sheet as a checklist.

PAIRED PRESENTATIONS

Tell the aliens . . .

Paired work is the easiest type of speaking frame presentation. Children who have previously used a 'talking partners' technique should adjust to using frames quickly; while for those who have not used the technique, the frames are an ideal introduction.

In the three *Tell the aliens . . .* activities, pairs of children develop and present a series of short talks involving clear description and explanation. The frames are couched in more formal 'literate language' than children generally use, and the need for complete clarity (so the aliens will understand) encourages them to use more explicit language. Children who are used to the restricted, implicit language of speech often feel that this level of description is 'stating the obvious', but such explicitness is essential for the understanding and communication of ideas in many areas of the curriculum:

- **Task 1:** *How it works* involves analysing and describing the characteristics of a familiar object, and explaining how it works.
- **Task 2:** *What it's like* involves describing a familiar item of clothing as explicitly as possible.
- **Task 3:** *How to play* involves analysing what is involved in playing a particular team game, and explaining the rules.

The activities give children the chance to hear appropriate 'literate language' patterns issuing from their own mouths, prior (it is to be hoped) to using them in written work, and to develop their control of technical terminology. They specifically cover these aspects of literate talk:

- speaking in complete sentences
- varying sentence construction (including a variety of sentence openings – adverbials, subordinate clauses)
- the standard English '. . . and I' (as opposed to 'Me and . . .')
- the language of exemplication (*For example, For instance* – more on page 52
- formal language use, including the use of the passive (*is used for . . . ; which is worn on . . . ; The game is played . . .*)
- techniques for defining technical terminology (e.g. *which is a . . . ; that is . . .* – more on page 54).

■ **Tell the aliens . . .**

Getting ready

1. Study the frame and decide what you are going to talk about. Make sure you know all the facts about it – or how you can find them out.

2. Read each section of the frame, and discuss how to finish it, so that it will be perfectly clear to an alien who has never seen such a thing. Jot down key words to remind you.

3. Practise your presentation together, taking turns to say one section each. Listen to each other and suggest improvements, e.g.
    *   more precise language
    *   extra detail
    *   clearer explanation.

4. When you are happy that your talk is perfect, practise until you can do it easily.

Introducing Paired Presentations

Children need training in order to work productively in pairs. When you start paired talk it is best to select the pairs yourself, choosing children you know will work well together. As children get used to the technique, they should be able to work with whoever happens to be sitting next to them.

- Display enlarged copies of the *Getting ready* notes and the relevant speaking frame.
- Read the frame with pupils. Explain that the aim is to develop explicit language – clear, precise description, which is needed in many cross-curricular tasks. If you assume that the aliens know absolutely nothing, you have to think very hard about how to describe familiar objects and processes.
- Explain that it will help if you have a visual aid (the thing you are describing, or posters illustrating it) which you can point to as you speak.
- Go through the *Getting ready* notes, and demonstrate each stage, working with a partner – another adult or an able child. Model the sorts of behaviour and outcome you are looking for, as in the 'points to watch for' boxes below.
- Give out small copies of the frame for pupils to work with.

Give the pairs an appropriate amount of time to decide exactly what they are going to say, and to rehearse it (if they need to check out facts, preparation will take longer). Watch how the pairs interact, and make sure they know you're watching. Tell them you won't necessarily intervene if things are not going well; they have to learn to work co-operatively, and can't always rely on you to sort out problems. You could use the assessment sheet on page 16 to focus on the work of some pairs.

Points to watch for during preparation	
Collaboration	Are they sharing tasks and ideas? Is one partner dominating? Have they found or made a visual aid?
Reflecting on content	Are they taking time talking through each section?
Refining ideas	Do their ideas develop, change, improve through discussion?
Note-making	Do notes cover key words for the presentation? Are both partners involved in making notes?
Practice	Do they practise? Do they use practice to improve content and presentation? Do they give useful feedback to each other?

Points to watch for in content	
Choice of topic	Is it a mutual choice? Is it suitable and interesting?
Accuracy/research	Are their statements/descriptions factually accurate? If necessary, are they able to find out more information?
Effectiveness	Are they providing the bare minimum response or looking for more engaging detail and means of expression?
Key words	Are they choosing good key words – brief and to the point?

Don't interrupt pupils who are doing well. Where you decide intervention is necessary, use questioning strategies to help them on course:

- *What's the problem here?*
- *If you don't agree, how can you find a solution?*
- *Where could you go to find a good word?*

Give positive feedback about the discussions at the end of the session, e.g.:

- *I liked the way Andrew and Asif shared their ideas.*
- *I liked the quiet voices these pairs used, so they wouldn't disturb others.*
- *I thought Maria and Shara were very clever to go and use the thesaurus.*

Then move straight into presentation – see pages 8–9.

■ **Tell the aliens . . .**

Giving the talk

1. Ensure that you know who is going to say each section, so you move fluently from one to the other.

2. When you are presenting, try to appear confident and in control.

- Look at the audience.
- Speak slowly, loudly and clearly enough for everyone to hear every word.
- Stand still, with good posture, and don't fidget.

If you look confident, you'll soon start to feel confident.

3. If anything goes wrong, try to get back on course without any fuss. Support your partner, and let your partner support you.

Staging Paired Presentations

Display an enlarged copy of the *Giving the talk* notes from page 8, and talk through them with pupils, drawing attention to the key points in the box. Choose a few pairs of children who are ready and ask them to present their talks while the class listens.

	Points to watch for in language
Sentence structure	Do they use the frame to speak in sentences? Does their expression indicate awareness of sentence boundaries? Are any extra sentences framed correctly?
Explicitness	Is the description clear and explicit? Have they added necessary detail?
Vocabulary	Is vocabulary varied or repetitive? Have they used precise nouns, suitable adjectives and verbs?
Standard English	Have they used the vocabulary and grammar of standard English?

	Points to watch for in presentation
Turn-taking/collaboration	Is their turn-taking organised or chaotic? Do they work together or as two individuals? If necessary, do they help each other out?
Pace	Is each speaker's delivery too fast or too slow?
Voice	Is each speaker audible? Are voices expressive or monotonous?
Audience engagement	Do they address the audience or each other? Do they use any visual aids effectively?
Body language	Do they stand confidently or self-consciously? Do they use gesture to enhance speech? Do they wriggle or fuss with their notes?
Dealing with problems	Are they easily distracted? If anything goes wrong, do they deal with it satisfactorily?

Give brief feedback to the pair on key points of their performance. Give specific praise wherever possible, e.g.:

- *I really liked the way you used 'object' or 'item' rather than 'thing'.*
- *You used the speaking frame very well, and your talk was all in good clear sentences.*
- *I loved the way you took turns, with each person's speech flowing on from the other's.*

Where feedback is negative, give it from the point of view of the audience, e.g.:

- *Sometimes it was difficult to hear because you were speaking very quickly.*
- *You have such a quiet voice we couldn't hear everything you said.*
- *I'm afraid I was distracted by the way you were fiddling with your paper.*

If you invite the rest of the class to comment on aspects of the performance (perhaps basing it on the *Giving the talk* notes), ensure that the criticism is constructive. As pupils become more experienced at giving paired presentations, feedback can become more detailed and specific.

If each presentation and feedback takes about five to eight minutes, you should be able to hear about six while still maintaining the interest of the class. Some pairs may also need more time to prepare. Provide further time as necessary, then give opportunities for all the pairs to present their talks, probably about six at a time. Each time, begin by revising the *Giving the talk* notes and reminding children of what they have learned from other pairs. Some pairs may wish to repeat their presentations in the light of what they learn – this should be encouraged.

 **Tell the aliens . . .**

How it works

.... and I are going to explain how a .... works.

> A .... is a type of .... which is used for ....

It usually consists of .... *detailed description* ....
....

> When you use a .... , you
> .... *detailed description* ....

The sort of person who would use a .... is a .... or ....

> For instance, ...

'Lewis and I are going to explain how a **screwdriver** works.

A **screwdriver** is a type of **tool** which is used for **fixing screws into place to hold things together** and also for **taking the screws out**.

It usually consists of **a long thin metal rod with a plastic handle at one end. At the other end the metal rod narrows into the correct shape to fit in the hole in the screw**. Sometimes the hole is like a slot and the screwdriver ends in a thin strip that fits the slot. On a Philips screw, it is more like a cross with four little slots, so the screwdriver ends in four little points to fit in the slots.

When you use a **screwdriver**, you **put the metal end into the hole in the screw**. Holding on to the handle, you turn the screwdriver round and round, and this turns the screw round. This either forces the screw into place, or loosens it out of the place it's in.

The sort of person who would use a **screwdriver** is a **carpenter, builder, maintenance worker or engineer**.

For instance, **a carpenter would use it when fixing two pieces of wood together with screws**.'

Talk about

- the importance of (a) choosing something simple; (b) understanding exactly how it works before trying to explain it.

- choosing an item to talk about, e.g.:

bottle opener	watch strap	key and lock
zip	light switch	clasp on a necklace or bracelet
paper clip	three-pin plug	pencil sharpener
elastic band	door catch	umbrella
scissors	sellotape dispenser	compass
stapler	mousetrap	egg timer

  You could give a list for pupils to choose from. Don't worry if several children choose the same item – the comparisons will be interesting.

- words that might fit into the second sentence, e.g. *tool, machine, utensil, mechanism*.

- what's important in describing such items (e.g. size, shape, design, functionality) and what's not particularly important (e.g. colour, pattern).

- thinking about how things work, and how to explain them.

- being very explicit – not worrying about 'stating the obvious'. Remember: aliens know nothing.

- the changes necessary if the item is plural, e.g. scissors, needle and thread. Use post-it notes to show the changes:

    .... **are** a type of .... **They** usually consist of ...., etc.

- changing *a* to *an* if the item begins with a vowel, e.g. elastic band, umbrella.

- using 'grown-up' language constructions and vocabulary, such as *container*.

- building up the description as you plan your talk.

 **Tell the aliens . . .**

What it's like
(an item of clothing)

.... and I are going to describe a ....

A .... is an item of clothing which is worn on ....

It usually consists of .... detailed description ....

....

.... are usually made of

....

They may have ....

The sort of person who would wear a ....
is .... For example, ...

....

12

'**Diamond** and I are going to describe a **blouse**.

A **blouse** is an item of clothing which is worn on **the upper part of the body.**

It usually consists of **a main part, which covers the body from the neck to below the waist, a collar for the head to go through, and armholes for the arms to go through. Many blouses also have two sleeves, which may be long or short. These come out of the armholes and cover the arms. Blouses without sleeves are called sleeveless blouses.**

Blouses are usually made of **cotton or a similar light-weight fabric, and may be plain or patterned.**

They may have **buttons or press studs to hold them together – these could be either on the front or the back of the blouse.**

The sort of person who would wear a **blouse** is **a woman or girl.** For example, **most schoolgirls wear blouses as part of their uniform.**'

Talk about

- choosing an item of clothing. Alert them to the possibilities, e.g.:

outdoor wear	school uniform	swimwear
nightwear	footwear	headgear
specialist clothing for soldiers, firefighters, bakers, etc.		

    Suggest they get or make visual aids to help with their talk.

- the sorts of detail to put into their description, e.g. shape, size, texture, weight, dimensions.

- thinking of all the possible variations and describing them too.

- specific 'scientific' vocabulary, e.g. *fabric, upper/lower body.*

- changes necessary if the item is plural, e.g. trousers, tights, leggings. Use post-it notes to show the changes:

    They usually **consist** of ....

- changing *a* to *an* if the item begins with a vowel, e.g. apron.

- building up the description as you plan your talk.

- ways in which the frame allows you to 'hedge your bets', e.g. *usually, they may have . . . .* Many written descriptions require this tentative language, as there are usually wide variations.

Tell the aliens . . .

How to play . . .

.... and I are going to explain how to play
.... , which involves two teams.
We shall call them Team A and Team B.

*The game is played .... where? ....
- that is a .... description ....*

In order to play you need ....
which is/are ....

To start the game, ...

Continue, exploring a step each, choosing suitable connectives, e.g.

If .... , ...

While ....

Then ....

When ....

The aim of the game is ....

14

'Imran and I are going to explain how to play **cricket**, which involves two teams. We shall call them Team A and Team B. **There are eleven players in each team.**

The game is played **on a cricket pitch** – that is a **large field covered in short grass with a section in the middle called the wicket. The wicket is a strip of very flat grass 22 yards long, and at each end there are three sticks, known as stumps. The sticks stand upright and across the top there are some little pieces of wood called bails.**

In order to play you need **the two sets of stumps, a small hard ball, and at least two cricket bats, which are like flat wooden clubs. You use these to hit the ball. You should also have a set of white clothes (shirt, trousers, cricket shoes with small studs in the bottom) and some protective clothing for batsmen and wicket keeper. The most important protective gear is the pads, which are padded covers for the legs, and the box, which you wear under your trousers to protect your private parts.**

To start the game, **Team A comes out on to the pitch – they will be bowling and fielding. Team B send out two batsmen, and one stands at each wicket. Then a bowler from Team A bowls the ball (an overarm throw) at the first batsman, trying to hit the wicket behind him. If he hits the wicket the batsman is out, and another batsman comes on instead of him. Other ways a batsman might be out include using his leg instead of his bat to defend his wicket (leg before wicket) or being caught (that is, he hits the ball and before it bounces one of the fielders catches it). On the other hand, if the batsman is able to hit the ball with the bat, and it goes far enough away for him to run right down the wicket and swap ends with his friend, that is called a run. Batsmen sometimes get two or three runs. If they hit the ball beyond the edge of the field (the boundary) without it touching the ground, they get six free runs, and if it touches the ground but still goes over the boundary, they get four free runs. When all the batsmen on Team B are out, they swap over and Team A bats.**

The aim of the game is **for one team to score more runs than the other.**'

Talk about

- choosing a game. It's important to choose a game you know well, e.g.:

  | football | rounders | hockey | basketball |
  | netball | relay race | rugby | five-a-side |

  Children may also be able to think of playground games involving teams.

- suggest they make or find visual aids to help with their talk – a plan of a football pitch and some pictures of the game in progress would be very helpful.

- the necessity of defining technical terminology (see pages 54–55). They need to become aware of the sorts of vocabulary that a non-enthusiast wouldn't know.

- summarising complex rules – explanations shouldn't drag on and on (practice is really important here).

Paired Presentations Assessment Sheet

Names ....   Date ....

....

Preparation	Presentation
Collaboration	Turn-taking and collaboration
Reflecting on content	Pace, volume, expression
Refining ideas	Engagement with audience
Note-making	Body language
Practice	Dealing with distractions/problems
Content	**Language**
Choice of topic	Sentence completion and organisation
Accuracy/research	Explicitness
Effectiveness	Vocabulary
Key words	Standard English

Suggestions for the types of behaviour to watch for are given on pages 7 and 9.

INDIVIDUAL PRESENTATIONS

In my opinion . . .

The individual *In my opinion . . .* presentations provide opportunities for children to give a short sustained talk on their own. We suggest using the paired activities first, to familiarise children with (a) the use of the frames and (b) speaking out to the class, because for some delivering a talk alone is a daunting task.

The *In my opinion . . .* talks provide opportunities for children to state an opinion and argue the case for it. They involve the use of persuasive language, delineation of the individual points in an argument, and disguising opinion to seem like fact:

- ***There should be a law:*** involves explaining an idea, thinking of three arguments to support it, and expressing these as clearly and cogently as possible.
- ***The greatest:*** involves choosing a personal hero or heroine, providing two reasons why this person is 'the greatest', anticipating a possible objection and refuting it.
- ***. . . should be banned:*** involves providing two arguments against an issue, anticipating an objection and refuting it.

These frames specifically cover these aspects of literate talk:

- the language of argument/justifying opinion (e.g. *I have two main reasons . . .*)
- connectives to delineate points (e.g. *First of all, Secondly, Finally*)
- ways of varying expression (e.g. *To begin with, First and foremost, First of all*)
- weasel words that disguise opinion as fact (*clearly, obvious advantage, it is clear that . . .*)
- conditionals and the subjunctive (e.g. *this law would improve, if this law were passed, other people might argue, perhaps some people would argue . . .*).

■ **In my opinion . . .**

Getting ready

1. Read the frame and choose a subject you care about. If necessary, spend a little time researching your subject.

2. Read each section of the frame and decide how to finish it. Jot down key words to remind you. Add extra sentences wherever necessary. Use persuasive language.

3. If it helps you sort out your thoughts, write your presentation out in full. However, the talk must be from memory or brief notes.

4. Practise your presentation, if possible to an audience – they may be able to help you improve it. Practise until you can do it easily.

Introducing Individual Talks

For each of the activities, give children plenty of time to choose their item and plan the talk in advance. Each activity makes an ideal homework exercise, but ensure that they are well prepared in class beforehand:

- Display enlarged copies of the *Getting ready* notes and the relevant speaking frame.
- Read and discuss the frame with pupils. Tell them that, if they wish, they can bring 'visual aids' to help with their talk, such as a picture or poster about their hero, etc.
- Go through the *Getting ready* notes and demonstrate each stage, modelling the sorts of behaviour and outcomes you want from the pupils (a completed frame is provided each time).
- When you come to practise the talk, get pupils to 'help' you by reading the sentence starts in chorus.
- Give out copies of the frame for pupils to work on.

Some children may want to compose and write out their entire talk. This is fine, but they should use the frame and notes (or an empty frame and memory) to deliver the talk, and not just read a 'prepared speech'. Some children may want to write and memorise their talk. This is also fine once in a while, as it helps develop auditory memory, but they should also do some talks *ex tempore*.

When observing pupils' preparation (or assessing or discussing their frames and notes before the talks), watch for the following areas. You could use the assessment sheet on page 28 to focus on the work of some children.

	Points to watch for during preparation
Reflecting on content	Does s/he take time to prepare or just rush at it?
Refining ideas	Does s/he draft and edit ideas? Does the talk grow over time?
Note-making	Do notes cover key words for the presentation? Are they too brief or too wordy?
Practice	Does s/he practise? How – by composing speech as writing? Practising to an audience? A mirror?

	Points to watch for in content
Choice of item	Is it a suitable and interesting choice? Is it a genuine choice or 'any port in a storm'?
Accuracy	Is the content factually accurate?
Effectiveness	Is the content interesting? Is there added detail and personal engagement?
Key words	Are the key words good ones? Has s/he noted any extra persuasive devices?

 **In my opinion . . .**

Giving the talk

Think about your audience – not yourself.

- Look at the audience. Talk directly to them. Give them a smile!

- If you have a visual aid, make sure they can see it. Point out anything significant that you mention in the talk.

- Speak slowly and clearly so they can hear. Pause slightly between sections. Speak up – don't mutter.

- If you look confident, the audience will believe in you – and you'll believe in yourself. So stand up straight, don't fidget, look professional!

If anything goes wrong, try to correct it without fuss.

Staging Individual Presentations

The logisitics of fitting 30-odd individual presentations into your classroom routine will depend on individual circumstances. If possible, aim for one or two half-hour sessions per day (for instance, at the beginning or end of the day). If children perform in groups of about six, it should be possible to get through the whole class's presentations in a week, devoting five to eight minutes to each child. If possible, ensure that the first couple of performers in each batch are fairly fluent readers and speakers. This allows less able pupils to familiarise themselves with the sentence frames and the sort of vocabulary and sentence patterns that are expected and appreciated.

You may wish to continue focused assessment of some pupils (see page 28), but during performances the teacher should be modelling how to listen appreciatively and provide positive feedback. The sheet could be filled in immediately after the presentation, or completed during the presentation by another adult.

	Points to watch for in language
Sentence structure	Does s/he use the frame to speak in sentences? Does expression indicate awareness of sentence boundaries (e.g. commas)? Are any extra sentences framed correctly?
Persuasion and argument	Is the language appropriate to the task? Are the arguments well expressed? Does s/he use any extra persuasive devices (e.g. rhetorical questions; appeals to the audience's emotions)?
Vocabulary	Is vocabulary varied or repetitive? Has s/he used precise nouns, suitable adjectives and verbs?
Coherence	Are there many intrusive 'ands'? Are conditional vern forms used consistently?
Standard English	Has s/he used the vocabulary and grammar of standard English?

	Points to watch for in presentation
Pace	Is delivery too fast or too slow?
Voice	Is speech audible? Is the voice expressive or monotonous? Does persuasive language sound suitably persuasive?
Audience engagement	Does s/he address the audience, maintaining eye contact?
Body language	Docs s/he stand confidently or self-consciously? Does s/he make good use of any visual aid? Does s/he fidget?
Dealing with problems	Is s/he easily distracted? If anything goes wrong, does s/he deal with it satisfactorily?

After thanking each child for his/her contribution, give at least one piece of positive feedback such as:

- *I liked the way you used the frame/adjusted the frame to your needs.*
- *That was a very thoughtful speech – you really made me think about the issue.*
- *I loved the way you gave that extra little bit of detail about . . . .*

Be very careful in giving negative feedback, as too much criticism could put shy children off speaking up. Focus on the difficulties you had as a listener, rather than those of the pupil as a speaker, helping the child recognise what is important in being heard and understood:

- *Could you give your first argument again – I didn't quite understand it.*
- *Could you tell me more about . . . ? I can't imagine it yet.*
- *Could you say the last bit a little slower – I didn't quite catch it.*

 **In my opinion . . .**

There should be a law

In my opinion, there should be a law that ....
....

This law would improve the quality of our lives in several ways. To begin with, it is clear that ....
....
....

Another obvious advantage of my law would be
....
....

Finally, most people would agree that if this law were passed, ...
....
....

I urge you to support my law!

'In my opinion, there should be a law that **teachers should get one year off teaching every seven years. This 'sabbatical year' would be on full pay, and the teacher would be expected to use it to improve his or her professionalism in some way.**

This law would improve the quality of our lives in several ways. To begin with, it is clear that **teaching is a very taxing and tiring profession. Just imagine being responsible for thirty children day in, day out! How long can someone do this job before they drop of exhaustion? If teachers were given regular breaks to recharge their batteries, they would be far better equipped to teach the rest of the time.**

Another obvious advantage of my law would be **that by improving their professionalism, they would become better teachers, with more to offer to their classes. They might use the sabbatical year for study, or research, or travel – and they'd return bubbling with ideas and enthusiasm. The quality of education in this country would soar.**

Finally, most people would agree that if this law were passed, **schools would become much happier places! Teachers wouldn't be tired, they'd have lots of new ideas, and they'd always have the next sabbatical to look forward to . . . Can you imagine how cheery and bright they'd all be? And happy teachers mean happy pupils!**

I urge you to support my law!'

Talk about

- the example above, if you can use it. In this case, a 'teacher's law' is chosen, written in a teacher's voice.

- choosing a new law. Suggest a few areas that children may be familiar with, such as:

children's rights	animal rights	education
anti-social behaviour	broadcasting	consumers' rights

- thinking about and around the issue: making sure you can think of three arguments in favour of it.

- how to explain and justify, using explicit organised sentences.

- the use of language in the frame to ensure that the three points are clearly delineated.

- persuasive devices they might use, e.g.:

  - rhetorical questions, e.g. *How long can someone do this job . . . ?*
  - emotive language, e.g. *exhaustion, bubbling with ideas, quality of education would soar*
  - expressions that 'turn opinion into fact', e.g. *It is clear that, another obvious advantage*
  - drawing audience along with you, e.g. *most people would agree that . . . .*

 **In my opinion . . .**

The greatest

In my opinion, the greatest person who ever lived is/was ....

There are two main points I want to make in support of this claim. First and foremost, ...
....

Secondly, ...

Other people might argue that ....
...., but I think they are wrong because ....

I hope you will agree that .... has done more for the world than anyone else in history.

'In my opinion the greatest person who ever lived was **William Shakespeare, the Elizabethan playwright.**

There are two main points I want to make in support of this claim. First and foremost, **Shakespeare's plays are brilliant and timeless. Have you ever thought how amazing it is that they are just as popular now as they were more than 400 years ago? And they were just as popular in Charles II's time, and Victoria's, and every generation. Not only that, but they are loved and performed in every country of the world, from America to Africa to China. Think how memorable his characters are – Macbeth, Hamlet, Romeo and Juliet. And how brilliantly he used language to bring them to life. No other artist has touched the hearts and minds of so many people.**

Secondly, **Shakespeare's contribution to the English language is greater than any other human being's. So many of the expressions we use every day come from his pen. He contributed countless words to the dictionary (incidentally, 'countless' was one of his) and helped to make the English language into an international treasure. Consider the many great writers this country has produced since Shakespeare! Dickens, Austen, J. K. Rowling! Shakespeare unlocked the language, and it's there for all of us to use. And now English is the international language, our greatest gift to the world. I believe that Shakespeare did more than anyone to make English what it is today.**

Other people might argue that **a playwright is not as important as a doctor, or a prophet, or a politican,** but I think they are wrong because **through his plays, Shakespeare helps to form people's minds. He can explain to us who we are and why we are like that – and his understanding is universal.**

I hope you will agree that **William Shakespeare** has done more for the world than anyone else in history.'

Talk about

- choosing a hero or heroine. Some children may want to choose a pop star or sporting hero. This is fine as long as they can provide arguments and state the case with enough enthusiasm.

- how to explain and justify, using explicit organised sentences.

- the use of language in the frame to ensure that the three points are clearly delineated (you could compare this with the language of *There should be a law* to demonstrate alternative constructions).

- persuasive devices they might use, e.g.:

  - rhetorical questions, e.g. *Have you ever thought . . . ?*
  - emotive language, e.g. *brilliant, timeless, memorable*
  - expressions that 'turn opinion into fact', e.g. *No other artist has . . .*
  - appealing to the audience along with imperative verbs, e.g. *Think how . . . Consider . . . .*

At the end of each group of presentations, you could

- invite questions or further points from the audience

- hold a vote for the most popular hero.

■ **In my opinion . . .**

. . . . should be banned

In my opinion, ... should be banned.

I have two main reasons for believing this.

First of all, as I'm sure you'll agree, ...
....

My second important reason for wanting to ban ....
.... is that ....
....

Perhaps some people would argue that ....
....

However, I would point out that
....

It is clear that a ban on ....
would be a great step forward!

'In my opinion, **junk mail** should be banned.

I have two main reasons for believing this. First of all, as I'm sure you'll agree, **it is a great waste of money. Apart from the stamp, there's the cost of the paper and printing – a single item of junk mail probably costs about 50p to produce. Think about how many 50ps that is, when they send their stupid letters to thousands of people. And have you ever thought about how all this is paid for? Why – by us, the customers! The costs of advertising are added to the costs of goods and services, so if there were no junk mail lots of things would be cheaper!**

My second important reason for wanting to ban **junk mail** is that **it is terribly wasteful of paper. Vast numbers of trees must be cut down to make enough paper for all the junk mail in the world, and then it's just thrown into people's bins, sometimes without even being opened. Surely we should be conserving our planet, not destroying it to create something completely pointless!**

Perhaps some people would argue that **junk mail keeps you informed about things you might want to buy.** However, I would point out that **it's better to have the exercise of going to the shops and seeing what's available. Anyway, you must agree that half the things you fancy in a catalogue aren't anywhere near as attractive when you see them in real life.**

It is clear that a ban on **junk mail** would be a great step forward!'

Talk about

- choosing something to ban. Suggest a few possible contenders, such as:

homework	school uniform	school
football	Literacy Hour	cabbage

- thinking about and around the issue: making sure you can think of three arguments in favour of it.

- how to explain and justify, using explicit organised sentences.

- the use of language in the frame to ensure that the three points are clearly delineated (you could compare it with the language of *There should be a law* and *The Greatest* to demonstrate alternative constructions).

  - persuasive devices they might use, e.g:
  - rhetorical questions, e.g. *Have you ever thought . . . ?*
  - emotive language, e.g. *stupid letters, vast numbers of trees*
  - drawing audience along with you, e.g .*I'm sure you'll agree, surely, you must agree*

At the end of each group of presentations, you could

- invite questions or further points from the audience

- hold a vote for the item they'd most like to ban.

Individual Presentations Assessment Sheet

Name .... **Date** ....

Preparation	Presentation
Approach to planning	*Use of speaking frame*
Reflecting on content	*Pace, volume, expression*
Refining ideas	*Engagement with audience*
Note-making	*Body language*
Practice	*Dealing with distractions/problems*
Content	**Language**
Choice of topic	*Sentence completion and coherence*
Accuracy/research	*Persuasion and argument*
Effectiveness	*Vocabulary*
Key words	*Standard English*

Suggestions for the types of behaviour to watch for are given on pages 19 and 21.

GROUP PRESENTATIONS

Compare and contrast . . .

The *Compare and contrast . . .* group presentations provide opportunities for two sorts of talk:

- collaborative talk within the group around the specific task – talk for learning
- participation in the formal presentation using the speaking frame – talk for writing.

Many thinking skills programmes are based on the first type of talk for learning: small group, open-ended discussion, in which pupils share and build on each other's ideas. The ideal size for a group in upper Key Stage 2 seems to be about five or six. Certainly there should be no more than six in a group.

However, for group discussion to be successful, the children need plenty of preliminary work to establish procedures and rules for behaviour. They should by now be familiar with speaking frames and how to use them, so the emphasis in the introduction to these *Compare and contrast . . .* activities is on developing (or revising) the ground rules of discussion. This discussion will involve decision-making about the comparisons or contrasts, and sharing out the sections for the eventual presentation. The final formal presentation is a further opportunity to familiarise children with literate language patterns – this time, the language frequently used in report writing.

The activities are designed to provide opportunities for shared creative thinking, involving:

- generating and evaluating ideas
- explaining and justifying ideas
- discussing, arguing a case and reaching agreement.

The final presentation involves shared responsibility, formal turn-taking, and speaking in complete sentences. While the group provides support, each child has an individual responsibility for their part in the performance, e.g. speaking clearly, adopting an appropriate speed and volume.

The frames specifically cover these aspects of literate talk:

- speaking in complete sentences, varying sentence construction
- ways of introducing a number of non-sequential points (*The first . . . , Another . . . , A further . . . , Finally . . .*)
- varying expression (*similar, alike, both, have in common*)
- explanatory and justificatory language.

**Compare and contrast . . .**

Rules for group discussion

Listen to others:

- look at the speaker
- try to remember what they say
- don't interrupt
- ask for further information if necessary.

Make sure everyone gets a chance to speak:

- shy people – be brave!
- bold people – don't hog the floor!

Always be polite – especially when you disagree!

Give reasons for what you say, e.g.

- 'I disagree because ....'
- 'I think .... because ....'

There are no wrong answers – just steps towards a solution.

Take turns to be secretary and make notes.

Introducing Group Discussion

Before asking children to work in groups on a specific task, spend time establishing the ground rules for behaviour. Ideally, pupils should devise these for themselves through class discussion, thus ensuring they have ownership of – and therefore greater commitment to – the final list. However, through guiding discussion, ensure they cover all the points listed on page 30.

Establish the rules firmly through class discussion, before asking the pupils to work in groups. Remember always to model the desired behaviour yourself during class discussion.

To introduce the *Compare and contrast . . .* activities:

- Display your *Rules for group discussion* and an enlarged copy of the relevant speaking frame.
- Read the frame with pupils. Discuss what is involved (see boxes below) and how the group might organise itself to create the presentation.
- Give a small copy of the frame to each group.

You could use the assessment sheet on page 00 to focus on the work of one or two groups.

Points to watch for during preparation

Collaboration	Are they working as a team? How did they allocate and share tasks? Is anyone left out or too dominant?
Reflecting on content	Is there genuine discussion, reflecting on content?
Refining ideas	Are they building on each other's ideas, making improvements?
Note-making	Do notes cover key words for the presentation? Is the secretarial system working? Is each child involved in making the notes for his/her section?
Practice	Do they use practice to improve content and presentation? Do they give useful feedback to each other?

Points to watch for in content

Creativity	How did they generate ideas? Are ideas too 'off-the-wall' or too 'stuck-in-the-mud'? Are they open-minded about all contributions?
Choice of ideas	How did they agree which ideas to use? Were the choices the best ones or too much influenced by group dynamics?
Effectiveness	Can they explain ideas clearly, and find arguments to justify them?
Key words	Are they choosing good key words – precise nouns and noun phrases, powerful adjectives and verbs?

Give positive specific feedback as for paired work on page 7.

Giving the talk

1. Make sure you know who is going to say each section. Stand in the right order.

2. Don't waste time between speakers. Swap quickly, so the presentation flows smoothly.

3. When it's your turn:
    *   look at the audience
    *   speak slowly, clearly and with expression
    *   stand and act confidently.

4. When it's not your turn, fade into the background:
    *   look down, or at the speaker
    *   don't make any sound
    *   don't do anything that might distract the speaker or audience.

5. If anything goes wrong, work as a team to sort it out.

Staging Group Presentations

If children are working in groups of six, it should be possible to stage all the presentations in one session. Display an enlarged copy of the *Giving the talk* notes on page 32, and talk through them with pupils, reminding them about general points they have learned about speaking in public.

Start with an able group, so the less able children have the chance to see a model before performing themselves. Use your feedback to the early groups to help others – if early presentations do not work well, it might be helpful to discuss the problems, and give groups a little longer to prepare.

Points to watch for in language

Sentence structure	Does their delivery indicate awareness of sentence boundaries? Are any extra sentences framed correctly?
Explicitness and argument	Are the points made explictly enough? Are explanations and arguments clear?
Vocabulary	Is vocabulary varied or repetitive? Have they used precise nouns, suitable adjectives and verbs?
Standard English	Have they used the vocabulary and grammar of standard English? Is there agreement in terms of tense, person, number?

Points to watch for in presentation

Turn-taking/collaboration	Is their turn-taking organised or chaotic? Are they working as a group? Is their performance organised or chaotic?
Pace	Is the pace of the presentation and of individual speakers satisfactory?
Voice	Is each speaker audible? Are voices expressive or monotonous?
Audience engagement	Do they address the audience or each other? Does their performance engage attention?
Body language	Does each speaker 'hold the floor' confidently? Do non-speakers fade back or attract attention?
Dealing with problems	Are they easily distracted? Do they work as a group to overcome problems?

At the end of each presentation, give brief feedback on key points of the performance, making praise specific wherever possible, e.g.:

- *I especially liked Andy's point because he explained it very clearly.*
- *Your turn-taking was excellent, so the talk flowed smoothly with no disruption between speakers.*
- *I liked the way you enunciated your words so clearly, so we could hear every word.*

Where feedback is negative, give it from the point of view of the audience, e.g.:

- *It was hard to concentrate on what Ben was saying because people were moving behind him.*
- *I didn't always understand your points because the explanations were a bit muddled.*
- *I'm afraid you lost me a bit because of the big gaps when you swapped over.*

If you invite the rest of the class to comment on aspects of the performance (perhaps basing it on the *Giving the talk* notes), ensure the criticism is constructive.

 **Compare and contrast . . .**

Compare

There are several ways in which .... and .... could be said to be similar.

The first way they are alike is that they are both

....

Another similarity is that they ....

....

A further feature they have in common is

....

Finally, they both ....

We think the most significant similarity is .... because ....

'There are several ways in which **a cup** and **a shoe** could be said to be similar.

The first way they are alike is that they are both **containers. The cup is a container for liquids and the shoe is a container for someone's foot.**

Another similarity is that they **are manufactured objects. Both are made in factories, and sold in shops.**

A further feature they have in common is **that they are small enough to be held in a human hand.**

Finally, they both **need regular cleaning. A cup must be washed after use, and a shoe needs polishing to keep it looking good.**

We think the most significant similarity is **that they are containers, because this is the point of their existence. Their size, the way they are made, and the need to clean them all depend on their function as containers.**'

For this activity, don't give a choice of items to compare. Present each group with two disparate objects – if possible, give them real things that they can handle and investigate. Coming up with four points of comparison is a useful thinking-skills activity, so practically any items will do.

Talk about

- obvious points of comparison, e.g. colour, consistency, origins, shape, size, function.

- the importance of explicitness and clarity in explanation and description (remind them of what they learned through the *Tell the aliens* activities).

- the sort of technical language that make descriptions sound 'grown-up' and professional, e.g. *container* as opposed to *holder for something*. Pupils may find a dictionary or thesaurus helpful in this respect.

- the 'grown-up' vocabulary in the frame: *a further feature* (instead of *another thing*); *significant* (instead of *most important*).

- varying language (e.g. *similar; are alike, similarity, have in common*).

This frame can be reused – for pairs, individuals or groups – whenever pupils are required to make comparisons, e.g. comparing characters, settings and plots in literature.

Compare and contrast . . .

Contrast

.... and ....
are different in a number of ways.

First of all, ...
but ....

Another difference is that ....,
while ....

Thirdly, ...
in contrast to ....
which ....

Finally, ...,
but ....

We think the most significant difference is ....
....
because ....

'A **cup** and **a shoe** are different in a number of ways.

First of all, **a cup is used for containing liquid,** but **a shoe is used for containing someone's foot.**

Another difference is that **a cup is usually made of china clay** while **a shoe is usually made of leather, fabric or plastic. Cups can also be made of plastic, but it is a different sort of plastic.**

Thirdly, **shoes have to be fairly flexible to allow the wearer's foot to move about,** in contrast to **cups,** which **are rigid. If they were flexible, the liquid might slosh about and spill out.**

Finally, **you wash cups in soapy water,** but **shoes are generally cleaned with a cloth and polish. If you washed leather shoes in soapy water, it would not do them any good at all.**

We think the most significant difference **between them is the material they are made from,** because **that affects other properties, like flexibility and washability.'**

Again, don't give a choice of items. Give the group two objects – they could be real objects to handle, or just named objects, places, characters. Coming up with four points of contrast is another useful thinking-skills activity.

Talk about

- obvious points of contrast, e.g. colour, consistency, origins, shape, size, function, material.

- the importance of explicitness and clarity in explanation and description (remind them of what they learned through the *Tell the aliens* activities).

- the use of the 'weasel word' *usually* to make a generalised statement.

- the sort of technical language that make descriptions sound 'grown-up' and professional, e.g. *flexible* as opposed to *bendy*. Pupils may find a dictionary or thesaurus helpful in this respect.

- the 'grown-up' vocabulary in the frame: *in contrast to, significant.*

This frame can be reused – by individuals, pairs or groups – whenever pupils have to look for differences, e.g. the difference between a playscript and a story, the differences between certain text-types.

Compare and contrast

In some ways, ... and .... are alike. For instance, they are both ....

....

> *Another feature they have in common is that*
>
> ....
>
> *Furthermore, they are both* ....

> However, they also differ in some ways. For example, ...,
> while ....

> Another difference is that ....
> whereas ....

> Finally, ...
> but ....

> On the whole, the similarities/differences seem more significant than the similarities/differences because.. .

'In some ways, **dogs** and **cats** are alike. For instance, they are both **four-legged animals.**

Another feature they have in common is that **they can both be domesticated and kept as pets.**

Furthermore, they are both **carnivorous.**

However, they also differ in some ways. For example, **dogs like to please their owners and to be with them whenever possible,** while **cats tend to live their own lives, and only bother with their owners when they feel like it.**

Another difference is that **dogs usually have to be taken out for exercise and kept on a lead,** whereas **cats come and go as they please, and don't need anyone to go with them.**

Finally, **dogs bark and whine, but cats meow and purr.**

On the whole, the similarities seem more significant than the differences because **they are more fundamental. The differences are just little things, but being a four-legged, carnivorous, domesticated animal is very particular similarity.'**

Again, don't give a choice of items. For this activity, you could choose any objects, places, people for each group to compare and contrast.

Talk about

• as the previous two activities.

This frame can be reused – by individuals, pairs or groups – whenever pupils have to look for differences, e.g. the difference between a playscript and a story, the differences between certain text-types.

Group Presentations Assessment Sheet

Group members ....

.... **Date** ....

Preparation	Presentation
Collaboration	*Turn-taking and collaboration*
Reflecting on content	*Pace, volume, expression*
Refining ideas	*Engagement with audience*
Note-making	*Body language*
Practice	*Dealing with distractions/problems*
Content	**Language**
Creativity	*Sentence completion and organisation*
Choice of ideas	*Language of argument*
Effectiveness	*Vocabulary*
Key words	*Standard English*

Suggestions for the types of behaviour to watch for are given on pages 31 and 33.

SIGNPOST SMORGASBOARD

These frames introduce common 'literate language' constructions for expressing key ideas (and the inter-relationships between ideas) which pupils will meet in literacy lessons and across the curriculum during Year 5.

The frames familiarise children with literate language through the opportunity to 'play around' with useful constructions orally. As well as introducing them to these language patterns (for both writing and speaking), the activities should develop thinking and communication skills in general, as access to suitable language can facilitate thought.

A lesson plan is provided for introducing each frame, although teachers may find that opportunities to use them crop up naturally in literacy lessons or other areas of the curriculum. Elements from the frames may also be used to create specific speaking frames for further paired, individual or group activities.

Illustrating punctuation

When using the speaking frames, ensure children are aware of punctuation (and its relationship to oral expression) by the use of visual symbols. Devise signals to represent commas and full stops, e.g.:

- comma – draw a large comma shape in the air with a finger
- full stop – jab the air with a finger.

Always use these when demonstrating the frames and ask pupils to use them when feeding back to the class.

Listen – imitate – innovate – invent

Some of the Smorgasboard pages contain frames that have appeared in the books for Years 3 and 4. Since a key element of the listen–imitate–innovate–invent system is the importance of repetition, important constructions need to be rehearsed every year. However, all the pages have been adapted for Year 5, usually by the addition of more complex vocabulary or constructions.

Cause and effect

When .... , _____ .

If .... , _____ .

.... , so _____ .

.... This causes _____ .

.... This means that _____ .

.... This results in _____ .

.... As a result, _____ .

.... Therefore _____ .

_____ because ....

The reason _____ is that ....

_____ due to ....

Cause and effect frames are included in all the *Speaking Frames* books because the constructions involved are so important. However, the page in this book contains three frames that do not appear in earlier books. Pupils who have played with these frames in earlier years will need no introduction and can go straight to using them to express their own cause-and-effect sentences. They may need their attention drawn to the three constructions in which there is a change to the verb form.

Introductory lesson

- Introduce the terms *cause* and *effect* and ensure children know what they mean. Point out that in the frames,

    Cause = ... Effect = _____

- Illustrate by completing the first frame using a cause/effect that is either

  – obvious (**When** *the window is open, it is cold.*)
  – silly (**When** *it is raining, Miss X turns into a parrot.*)

  Indicate the point where the comma separates the two chunks by drawing a large comma in the air with your finger.

- Ask pupils to fill the same cause and effect into the next six frames, indicating the comma in the same way.

    If *it is raining, Miss X turns into a parrot.*
    It is raining, **so** *Miss X turns into a parrot.*
    It is raining. **This causes** *Miss X to turn into a parrot.* (Note change in verb form.)
    It is raining. **This means that** *Miss X turns into a parrot.*
    It is raining. **This results in** *Miss X turning into a parrot.* (Note change in verb form.)
    It is raining. **Therefore** *Miss X turns into a parrot.*

- Point out that, sometimes, the effect is stated before the cause:

    Miss X turns into a parrot **because** *it is raining.*
    The reason *Miss X turns into a parrot* **is that** *it is raining.*
    Miss X has turned into a parrot **due to** *the rain.* (Note changes.)

- You may wish to point out that in the first two frames, the chunks can be reversed:

    Miss X turns into a parrot **when** *it is raining.*
    Miss X turns into a parrot **if** *it is raining.*

- Ask pupils in pairs to think up their own cause and effect and take turns to fit it into the frames (remind them of the verb changes with *This causes*, *This results in* and *due to*). Ask a number of pupils to feed back their results to the class, starting with more able pupils, so that the less able hear the model a few times before trying it themselves.

Sequence of events

Firstly, . . .	Finally, . . .
First of all	Eventually, . . .
To start with	At last, . . .
To begin with . . .	At the end, . . .
Secondly, . . .	Next . . . .
After that . . .	Then . . .

When . . . , . . .   Since . . . , . . .

After . . . , . . .   Before . . . , . . .   Until . . . , . . .

While . . . , . . .   As . . . , . . .   Meanwhile . . . , . . .

This exercise is useful preparation for story writing, or cross-curricular writing of recount, instruction or explanation text. These constructions have been introduced in earlier books, but need frequent revisiting to ensure children have a wide range of 'sequencing signposts'.

Introductory lesson

- Introduce the term *sequence of events* and ensure that children know what it means. Point out that:
    - the words in the first column are ways of starting a sequence
    - those in the second are for the middle of a sequence
    - the last column shows words that can conclude a sequence

    Any word can be chosen from any column so there are many possible permutations, e.g.

    Firstly, . . .   *After that . . .*   *At the end . . .*

    However, certain forms of words are sometimes more appropriate than others, depending on the sentence.

- Illustrate writing a sequence of three events on the board, e.g. a morning at school up to break time: *We take the register. We have a maths lesson. We go out for break.* Then select three suitable words or phrases from the lists and say the sentences with them in place:

    First of all *we take the register.* **Next** *we have a maths lesson.* **Finally,** *we go out for break.*

    Indicate any commas by drawing them in the air with your finger. Ask pupils to try alternative words and phrases, discussing whether they 'sound right'.

- Point out that in sequences of more than three events, you can use extra connectives from the central column, avoiding repetition (one *Then* is fine; more than one sounds dreary). Add in another event:

    First of all *we take the register.* **Next** *we have a maths lesson.* **Later** *we have half an hour's reading.* **Finally,** *we go out for break.*

- Demonstrate that the constructions beneath the line can be used anywhere:

    When *school starts, we take the register.*
    After *the register, we have a maths lesson.*
    Next *comes half an hour's reading* **until** *the bell goes for break.*

- Ask pupils in pairs to think up a simple sequence of events, e.g. things you do when you get up in the morning, when you get home from school or when you eat your packed lunch. They should then try expressing it in as many different ways as possible, varying connectives to achieve different effects. If they note down each sequence of connectives, some pairs can feed back their efforts to the rest of the class.

Adding information

as well   too

Also . . .

Furthermore, . . .

Moreover, . . .

In addition, . . .

What is more, . . .

A second/third reason is . . .

Another point is . . .

A further argument is . . .

Finally, . . .

Earlier books in this series introduce a limited number of ways a speaker or writer can add to information. This activity builds on these, and includes constructions for adding point on point, argument on argument, and reason on reason. This is such a common requirement in writing and speech that children's language use benefits enormously if they have a range of constructions available (instead of the ubiquitous *and*).

Introductory lesson

- Talk about how the word *and* is often over-used. While it is fine to use it occasionally, written work can be much improved by learning and using a variety of connectives.

- Write up two facts which can be linked by *and,* e.g.:

  Transport improved in Victorian times. There were many new inventions.

  Demonstrate orally how the sentences can be linked by *and* and by the other devices:

  *Transport improved in Victorian times **and** there were many new inventions.*
  *Transport improved in Victorian times. There were many new inventions **as well**.*
  *Transport improved in Victorian times. There were many new inventions **too**.*
  *Transport improved in Victorian times. **Also** there were many new inventions.*
  *There were **also** many new inventions.*
  *Transport improved in Victorian times. **Furthermore** there were many new inventions.*
  *Transport improved in Victorian times. **Moreover,** there were many new inventions.*
  *Transport improved in Victorian times. **In addition**, there were many new inventions.*
  *Transport improved in Victorian times. **What is more**, there were many new inventions.*

- Ask children in pairs to do the same with another two facts linked by *and*, perhaps related to recent reading or cross-curricular work. The second fact must be purely additional information (children often use *and* instead of causal or time connectives) so they will have to experiment until they find two facts that work.

- Ask children to feed back their sentences, joined in different ways. Ask which they like the best each time. Perhaps you could take a vote on it.

- On another occasion, use the sentence starts in the box to illustrate how to build an argument without repetition, e.g.:

  *The reason I am in favour of television is that it has many entertainment programmes. **A second** reason is that we can watch important sporting events. **Another** point is that it keeps everyone up to date with the news. **A further** argument is that it is often educational. **Finally**, it lets you watch films in your own home.*

  Help children to see that *Also, Furthermore, What is more, In addition* could also be substituted here.

- Ask pairs to list arguments for or against something, and then to practise them orally, using a variety of connectives.

These frames can be used when children are expressing their views about fiction or topics across the curriculum.

Opposing information

but   yet

while   although

whereas

However . . .

Nevertheless . . .

On the other hand, . . .

Despite this, . . .

---

or

Alternatively,

These frames introduce children to alternative ways of saying *but*. A few of these constructions will be familiar from earlier books, but this collection is much wider and more diverse than anything covered previously.

Introductory lesson

- Talk about the word *but* and how it introduces an opposite fact or point of view. You could represent this opposition with the symbol >< . In formal writing, *but* should never be used to start a sentence (it is a co-ordinating conjunction, which technically should always come *between* two chunks of meaning). Pupils therefore need an alternative to *but* for use in their writing and speech.

- Write up two facts which can be linked by *but*, e.g.:

  I like tomato sauce. I hate tomatoes.

  Ask pupils to demonstrate orally how these sentences can be linked by *but* and the other devices:

  *I like tomato sauce **but** I hate tomatoes.*
  *I like tomato sauce **yet** I hate tomatoes.*
  *I like tomato sauce **while** I hate tomatoes.*
  *I like tomato sauce **although** I hate tomatoes.*
  *I like tomato sauce **whereas** I hate tomatoes.*
  *I like tomato sauce. **However,** I hate tomatoes.*
  *I like tomato sauce. **Nevertheless** I hate tomatoes.*
  *I like tomato sauce. **On the other hand,** I hate tomatoes.*
  *I like tomato sauce. **Despite this,** I hate tomatoes.*

- Ask pupils in pairs to try linking the following pairs of facts with each of the connectives:

  My friend likes football. I prefer cricket.
  James is a boy. Zoe is a girl.

  As pairs report back, ask the class which versions they like and dislike, and why.

- *But* is a very versatile word and some of the suggested connectives cannot be substituted for all uses of it. Ask children in pairs to search for *but* in texts in the classroom and try substituting the other words. Then, during feedback, discuss which ones work in terms of conveying meaning and which don't. You should find that *However* can almost always be substituted.

- On another occasion, look at the use of *but* in providing alternatives. Provide two statements that offer a choice, e.g.:

  James could go to the cinema. He could stay at home.

  and let children link them with *but, yet, while, However, On the other hand.* This time add in *or* and *Alternatively.* Discuss which sound the best.

- Ask pairs of pupils to try the same with other alternative statements:

  It might rain. It might be sunny.
  We can make a sandwich. It might be fun to have a takeaway.

Generalisation

probably   possibly

arguably   on the whole

perhaps   maybe

usually   generally   mostly

may   might   could tend(s) to   seem(s) to

about   around   circa

approximately   roughly

This frame is new for Year 5. It provides a selection of words and phrases that can be used to introduce generalisations or approximations in descriptive writing. These are important in factual writing to 'cover' the writer when a point is not (or might not be) absolute. They are also used frequently in persuasive writing, where they are sometimes known as 'weasel words' (e.g. '*Probably* the best lager in the world').

Introductory lesson

- Discuss the fact that some 'statements of fact' may be debatable, e.g. *Fish feel no pain when they are caught.* With pupils, try out each of the words above the box (some may be possible in more than one position). Ask pupils to listen to each construction and decide which they think 'sounds right'.

  > **Probably** *fish feel no pain when they are caught.*
  > *Fish* **probably** *feel no pain when they are caught.*
  > **Possibly** *fish feel no pain when they are caught.*
  > **Arguably** *fish feel no pain when they are caught.*
  > **On the whole,** *fish feel no pain when they are caught.*
  > **Perhaps** *fish feel no pain when they are caught.*
  > **Maybe** *fish feel no pain when they are caught.*
  > **Usually** *fish feel no pain when they are caught.*
  > **Generally** *fish feel no pain when they are caught.*
  > **Mostly,** *fish feel no pain when they are caught.*

- You can also make a generalisation by the use of 'tentative' verbs. Ask pupils to try inserting the verbs from the box, e.g.

  > *Fish* **may** *feel no pain when they are caught.*
  > *Fish* **might** *feel no pain when they are caught.*
  > *Fish* **could** *feel no pain when they are caught.*
  > *Fish* **tend to** *feel no pain when they are caught.*
  > *Fish* **seem to** *feel no pain when they are caught.*

- Through discussion, establish that in this case *On the whole, Usually, Generally, Mostly* and *tend to* are inappropriate, as we don't know for sure one way or the other. But they may work for another debatable statement, e.g. *Boys are better at football than girls.* It is as well to have access to a wide range of vocabulary, so you can pick and choose (and vary your expression).

- Ask pupils in pairs to make up a debatable statement of their own. They should then go through the words, trying each out, and select the three they like best in their sentence.

- Ask a pair of pupils to feed back their best three sentences. Ask other pupils to try some of the other constructions and discuss why the pair rejected them. Repeat with a number of pairs, so that the class is exposed to frequent repetition of the 'weasel words'.

- On another occasion, look at the words below the box. These words allow you to give an approximation, particularly when you are dealing with numbers, e.g. *The woman was 25 years old: about 25, around 25, approximately 25, roughly 25, circa 25.* Discuss which 'sounds the best' in this and other sentences. Help them recognise that *approximately* is mainly used in scientific writing, and *circa* is often used in history for dates.

Revisit these frames when pupils are about to write report, persuasion or discussion texts, to rehearse the constructions orally.

Giving examples

For example, . . .

For instance, . . .

such as . . .   e.g. . . .

including . . .

like . . .

An example of this is . . .

An illustration of this is . . .

This can be illustrated by . . .

This is a new frame for Year 5, providing a variety of ways of introducing examples. Exemplification is required in all types of writing, but particularly in reports and persuasive writing. Many children introduce examples with the term *like*, which is frequently inelegant and sometimes grammatically incorrect.

Introductory lesson

- Discuss why it is sometimes necessary to give examples

  - to back up a point
  - to clarify a description
  - sometimes instead of a definition or explanation.

- Provide an example, and try it with each, e.g.:

  There are many breeds of dog. **For example**, *there are large dogs like the Great Dane, and small dogs like the Yorkshire terrier.*
  There are many breeds of dog. **For instance**, *there are large dogs like the Great Dane, and small dogs like the Yorkshire terrier.*
  There are many breeds of dog, **such as** *large dogs like the Great Dane, and small dogs like the Yorkshire terrier.*
  There are many breeds of dog, **e.g.** *large dogs like the Great Dane, and small dogs like the Yorkshire terrier.*
  There are many breeds of dog, **including** *large dogs like the Great Dane, and small dogs like the Yorkshire terrier.*
  There are many breeds of dog, **like** *large dogs like the Great Dane, and small dogs like the Yorkshire terrier.*

  Establish that *like* and *such as* are unsuitable here.

- Establish that certain constructions fit certain situations, e.g.:

  You should choose a dog to suit your lifestyle. **For example**, *city dwellers should not buy a dog that needs lots of exercise* will work with **For instance** and **e.g.** but with none of the others.

- Ask pupils in pairs to look in non-fiction books to find places where the author has given an example, e.g. *Rules for group discussion* on page 30 and try substituting the other constructions, to find those that work and those that don't work. Ask pairs to report back, and establish that some constructions work better for lists, and others for single specific examples.

Revisit these frames when pupils are about to write report, persuasion or discussion texts, to rehearse the constructions orally. Display them as part of the 'writing toolkit' when pupils are writing.

Giving definitions

_____, which is . . .

_____ . This is . . .

_____ (.....................................)

.... called _____

.... known as _____

_____ who ....

This is a new frame for Year 5, providing a variety of ways of embedding definitions in the body of a text. This is frequently necessary in non-fiction writing, where technical terminology is introduced.

Introductory lesson

- Discuss how it is often necessary to define the terms you use when writing non-fiction, especially if they are technical terms that the general reader may not know, e.g. *The butterfly feeds through its <u>proboscis</u>,* **which** *is a tube on the front of its head.*

  Explain that in each of our speaking frames, the technical term is represented by a straight line and the definition by a dotted line.

- Write up the example and ask pupils to try substituting the other constructions:

  The butterfly feeds through its <u>proboscis</u>. **This** *is a tube on the front of its head.*
  The butterfly feeds through its <u>proboscis</u> **(a tube on the front of its head)**.
  The butterfly feeds through a tube on the front of its head **called** *a <u>proboscis</u>.*
  The butterfly feeds through a tube on the front of its head **known as** *a <u>proboscis</u>.*

- Point out that when you are defining or describing a human being, the introductory word is *who* as opposed to *which*, e.g.:

  The knight was served by his <u>squire</u>, **who** *was usually a young boy training to be a knight.*

  Ask pupils to try substituting all the other constructions.

- Help pupils to recognise also that when the definition is plural, *This* has to change to *These,* e.g.
  . . . squires. ***These*** *were usually . . .*

- Ask pupils in pairs
  - either to think up a sentence including a technical term, which they can define
  - or to find an example in non-fiction books and to try substituting the other constructions. Ask pairs to report back, so that pupils gain familiarity with all the frames.

Revisit these frames when pupils are about to write any non-fiction texts in which technical terminology occurs, to rehearse the constructions orally. Display them as part of the 'writing toolkit' when pupils are writing.

Summing up

so I/we conclude ....

I/we therefore conclude ....

This leads me/us to conclude ....

believe	think
feel	agree

On the whole,... .

Overall,... .

In conclusion,... .

Taking everything into account ... .

After due consideration,... .

56

This frame is new for Year 5. It provides a selection of words and phrases that can be used at the end of a persuasion or discussion text, when the author presents his/her final conclusions.

Introductory lesson

- Discuss the meaning of *conclusion* in the context of persuasion and discussion text (i.e. deciding on a point of view after weighing all the evidence and arguments). Give an example, e.g. **On the whole**, *the arguments in favour of homework seem to outweigh those against,* **so** *I do not think it should be banned.*

- Explain that the two sets of frames are interchangeable, as are the four alternatives to the verb *conclude* in the box on the right. Write up your example and ask pupils to try substituting the other frames, to see how many different ways they can express a final conclusion. Have some pairs feed back to the class so they all become familiar with the constructions.

- Ask pupils in pairs to

  - imagine another debatable topic, e.g. *foxhunting,*
  - decide on whether the arguments **for** or **against** would win
  - fill in the frames appropriately
  - try as many substitutions as they can.

  Ask some pairs to feed some of their completed frames back to the class.

Revisit these frames when pupils are about to write persuasion or discussion texts, to rehearse the constructions orally. Display them as part of the 'writing toolkit' when pupils are writing.

Evidence from the text

This is illustrated on page .... , where

....

We know this because on page .... the author says

....

The evidence for this is on page .... where

....

The words that tell us this are ....
on page ....

On page ...., the author says ....
This suggests that ....

indicates	implies	shows

Simpler versions of some of these frames appear in the *Speaking Frames* books for Years 3 and 4. They introduce the importance of evidence, especially in reading, to help children justify their inferences. Critical reading – 'interrogating the text' – is a good preparation for critical thinking in general, and thus intellectual good health. All children are capable of critical thought, but articulating reasons for opinions and impressions is not easy, so the more help we can give, the better.

Introductory lesson

- Introduce the term *evidence* (proof) and talk about why it is important to provide evidence for our impressions.

- Use an example of inference from your current reading, and provide the evidence. Ask children to use each of the speaking frames to express it. Explain that the verbs in the box at the bottom of the page may be substituted for *suggests* in the final frame, depending on which seems most appropriate for the particular point. All these words are useful for children to have in their repertoire when providing evidence, so it's worth giving many opportunities for practice. (Note: another word frequently used in this context is *infers*. This actually means 'draws the conclusion', so it is the reader who infers something from the text. This meaning is gradually changing because of usage, but at present it's probably still worth discouraging children from using it.)

- Set another question relating to current reading (or a number of questions for different groups) and ask pupils to discuss in pairs, find the evidence, and express it using each of the frames. In feedback, ensure that they hear each of the frames several times.

This set of frames can be used frequently during shared and guided reading to help children formulate and articulate the reasons behind their responses to texts.

USEFUL RESOURCES

Skeleton Poster Books (and OHTs) Sue Palmer: TTS (0800 318686)

How to Teach Writing Across the Curriculum at Key Stage 1 Sue Palmer: David Fulton Publishers

How to Teach Writing Across the Curriculum at Key Stage 2 Sue Palmer: David Fulton Publishers

How to Teach Story Writing at Key Stage 1 Pie Corbett: David Fulton Publishers

How to Teach Fiction Writing at Key Stage 2 Pie Corbett: David Fulton Publishers

Jumpstart! Literacy Games and Starters Pie Corbett: David Fulton Publishers

Big Book Grammar Sue Palmer and Michaela Morgan: Heinemann

Skeleton Poster Books for Grammar (and OHTs) Sue Palmer: TTS (0800 318686)

Exploring the Writing of Genres Beverly Derewianka: UKRA (01763 241188)

Connections (cross-curricular literacy resources) Sue Palmer, series editor: Oxford University Press

Tell Me: Children Reading and Talking Aidan Chambers: Thimble Press

Thinking Allowed (video and booklet) Queens School, Richmond-on-Thames (0208 940 3580)

The English Speaking Board (assessments in spoken English) 01704 501730

Literacy: What Works? Sue Palmer and Pie Corbett: Nelson Thornes

The author would be very grateful for feedback on the use of speaking frames in the classroom. Please make contact via e-mail: sue@suepalmer.co.uk